Innovative
BEADED JEWELRY
Techniques

Innovative
BEADED JEWELRY
Techniques

Gineke Root

LACIS
PUBLICATIONS
Berkeley, California 94703

Translated from the Dutch title
KRALEN GEREGEN TOT SIERADEN
Originally Published by
Cantecleer bv, de Bilt

© 1988 Uitgeverij Cantecleer bv, de Bilt
© 1994 English text, Kangaroo Press

Photography: Hans van Ommeren, Woerden
Diagrams: Gineke Root and Michel D. Walvisch, Heemstede
Design: Karel van Laar, de Bilt
English translation: Tina Llowarch, Kenthurst

Reprinted 1995 and 1997
This edition published 1994 by
LACIS PUBLICATIONS
3163 Adeline Street
Berkeley, California 94706

ISBN 0-916896-60-9

Acknowledgments

My thanks to:
Several artists whose work has been
offered for use in this publication:
Hans van Ommeren, who so artistically
photographed all the jewelry,
Michel Walvisch, who helped me with the
drawings,
Thomas Nicholas, for his assistance,
Edwin and Sanne Walvisch,
and to everyone who in any way inspired
or helped me in the making of this book.

Publisher's Note

Reflecting the international interest in
beadwork, the publisher acknowledges
the British spelling of *jewellery* and *colour*
which are used throughout the text rather
than the accepted spelling of *jewelry* and
color in the US.

Contents

1 Introduction 6

2 Beads and sequins 7

3 Essential equipment 10
Nylon thread 10
Beading needles 10
Pliers 10

4 Finishing 10

5 Flat beading 12
Necklace 14

6 Simple circular beading 15
Beaded cord necklace 16

7 Beaded loops 19
Simple twist necklace 20
Variation of simple twist necklace 21
Diabolo necklace 24
Brooch, variation of diabolo 25
Spiral necklace 25
Earrings, variation of spiral 29
Necklace, variation of spiral 29
Long bugle beads necklace, stepped 30
Long bugle beads necklace with central
motif 32
Necklace with pearls 32
Necklace with sequins 33
Brooch, large twist 34
Lapel or hat pin, large twist 34
Large twist necklace 39

8 Other beading 39
Earrings, beadballs 39
Necklace, variation of beadballs 39
Beaded loop earrings 42
Earrings 42
Bracelet 46
Lizard brooch 47
Simple collar 50
Pierrot neckpiece 52

1 Introduction

Beads have attracted attention for thousands of years. Today they may be collected for their beauty of composition, for their variety of colours, or just because someone might want to use them one day. Everybody has occasions where dressing up with beads is called for. All sorts of materials have been used all over the world to make beads and sequins for jewellery and decoration.

Anyone who can string beads together can work with them. Making beaded jewellery and decorations is a relaxing and easily mastered craft.

Beading can be just stringing beads together onto cotton, which can be quite inspiring. It can also be a little more intricate — beading can be done in a flat piece or worked in a circular or tube shape.

In circular beading, the beads are threaded one after the other and are then stitched through an existing bead. This occurs always in the same direction and in the form of a spiral (see Chapter 6). New beads are introduced and fastened with the same thread to the beaded piece, eventually forming a tubular beaded string.

Spiral beading is done by beading in a circle in a continuing circular motion, without closing each separate circle.

For flat beading, bead after bead is threaded and fastened in a backward and forward direction, creating a ribbon of beads.

The possibilities of beading are limitless. Beads are available in all sorts of shapes, sizes and colours; older beads (e.g. from old jewellery) can be tastefully combined with new beads. Each pattern can be made original and very individual with new ideas and variations. Every craft shop has its own assortment of beads and it can be very rewarding and exciting to gather an assortment of beads together.

The stringing together of beads is a very old technique. The circular beading and the different combinations and patterns described in this book are authentic and are used by many beading enthusiasts. Beaded jewellery can be brilliantly combined with crocheted and supple bead cords, knitted bead balls and such like.

2 Beads and sequins

Almost every sort of bead and sequin is suitable for jewellery beading in a myriad combinations of colours, varieties, sizes and shapes. There are so many ways of putting beads together for jewellery that the possibilities seem endless. You can create something suitable for any occasion.

Sequins, which are made from synthetic materials, combine very effectively with beads. There are beads made from glass and metal and all sorts of artificial materials in all colour combinations, shapes and sizes. Beads of wood, porcelain and ceramic are not quite as suitable for jewellery, wooden beads not always being colourfast and beads of porcelain and ceramic being often too heavy for this kind of lightweight beading. They can, however, be used as an extras for decorating or fastening a finished piece.

Check for the colourfastness of the beads and sequins you wish to use. The so-called painted and coloured pearls, for example, are not always colourfast and the same goes for glass beads with an infusion of another colour. Silver and gold coloured beads that like pearls have been dipped in a paint bath can lose their colour and shine very quickly. Do make a point of checking colourfastness to prevent disappointment.

Colour choice is a very personal thing which depends on the colour of the clothes that the jewellery is to be worn with. The colours of the beads influence each other strongly; sometimes they have a very surprising effect on each other, which can make beading very exciting. Several shades of one colour could be used together, for example, beige, light brown, middle brown and dark brown, or contrasting colours, such as red and black.

When through the choice of colour or bead type a piece of jewellery becomes too neutral or too boring — for example where different shades of the one colour have been used — the article can be lifted by using a contrast colour (such as silver or gold) or beads of a different material or shape.

The colours of transparent beads can appear to run into each other. Harsh contrasting effects can be softened by the addition of transparent beads. Although the so-called oil beads, transparent, shining and enamelled glass or synthetic beads can create extra detail in a beaded article, too many beads of this type can give an untidy or overstated effect. Naturally this will depend entirely on your own personal taste.

Round, dull, nonporous beads, even if contrasted with rich colours in a piece of jewellery, can sometimes become lacklustre or boring. Combining them with transparent oil beads can bring an article back to life again.

The ultimate choice of colours or combinations of colours in a design will be uniquely yours. Remember that glass beads tend to be heavier than synthetic or metal beads.

The many different varieties, shapes and sizes of beads include:
• Rocailles or seed beads, small round, regular shaped shiny glass or synthetic beads (2 to 3 mm). Because of their uniform shape and the fact that they can be beaded flat and close together, they are very suitable for embroidery or flat beading.
• Faceted beads, which have many-sided cuts, are made in glass or synthetic materials and in a variety of shapes and sizes (2, 3, 4, 5 and 6 mm).

• Bugle beads are glass or synthetic beads in the form of tiny tubes (2-3 mm). Glass beads can have sharp or hooked edges which can damage the nylon beading thread. If you can't avoid using very sharp bugles, it may be advisable to work with a nylon coated wire.
• Large rocailles are evenly shaped glass or synthetic beads (4, 5 or 6 mm).
• Large bugle beads are glass or synthetic beads in the shape of a longer tube in a variety of lengths and thicknesses (4, 5 or 6 mm). These bugle beads can also have very sharp edges, which needs to be taken into account when using them.
• Oval shaped beads of glass or synthetic materials (4-5 mm).
• Painted and coloured synthetic pearls in different sizes.
• Metal beads come in silver or gold colours, round or faceted in different sizes.
• Metal decorative beads come in silver or gold colours, in different shapes and sizes. The so-called Indian beads are often very unusual and striking in shape, structure or design. They can be used in combination with strass beads to decorate a piece of jewellery.
• Strass beads are cut glass stones set in a silver or gold metal setting and come in a variety of shapes and sizes (rondelle).
• Flat cabochons can be smooth or decorated and are available in different shapes and sizes.
• Hollow cabochons can be smooth or decorated and are also available in different shapes and sizes.
• Synthetic decorative beads are smooth or decorated transparent beads and are very suitable to be used as the kernel for bead balls. They are available in different sizes and are very lightweight.

The hole in the centre of a bead must generally be large enough to allow the needle and thread to be passed through at least twice. This does not apply to leader beads or basic column beads, which can be small beads with small holes.

Watch for sharp and poorly finished glass beads which will cause the thread to wear very quickly. They are not really suitable for making jewellery. To have the thread break while while you are working causes great inconvenience and disappointment. Beads come in many different weights and sizes. When a pattern stipulates a certain amount of beads by weight, variations in numbers are possible because of varying sizes and weights. If you are unsure, buy extra so you will sufficient beads to finish the pattern. If you have to buy more you may occasionally find that the ones you want are sold out or not of the same dye lot, which could result in a new batch of beads being a totally different colour. New beads continually become available. Building up an assortment of colours and shapes to make your own personal jewellery can become quite addictive!

>1 *Various essentials*

3 Essential equipment

Nylon thread

Beads are threaded very close together up against each other so that the thread becomes almost invisible, yet it is the mainstay of the basic beadwork. The work must be strong yet remain supple; in general use nylon thread of approximately 0.20 mm is best. This thread is easy to use, stays supple and doesn't stretch too much. When working to a pattern that uses larger beads a thread of approximately 0.25 mm could be used. A doubled thread can also be used for extra strength, but remember the emphasis is on keeping the beading work supple.

Nylon thread is available from craft shops. Fine fishing line is also suitable.

Beading needles

These needles are available in a variety of lengths and thicknesses in craft shops.

They are mostly long and thin with a small eye that allows for the nylon thread to pass through the bead easily. A useful trick for threading a needle is to pinch the end of the thread very hard with flat-nosed pliers and cut a small piece off the end. This makes the end of the thread thinner and more easily threaded through the needle. Hold the needle between thumb and forefinger and push the needle over the end of the thread.

Pliers

Using the right equipment makes beading much easier.

Flat-nosed and round-nosed jeweller's pliers give a professional finish to your jewellery when you are adding caps and eyepins.

4 Finishing

The finish of the jewellery is very important. It must be done meticulously, with all starting and finishing threads knotted and invisibly worked back into the beaded work. The finish must be strong and durable to prevent the piece of jewellery from falling apart while it is being worn. Clasps can add an attractive extra decorative touch to the beading. They must be strong enough and securely attached to hold the piece of jewellery together. Bead shops usually have quite a variety of silver and gold dipped or plated clasps. Jewellers also have some beautiful, but probably more expensive, clasps.

Flat beaded jewellery can be finished with a flat clasp, buckle or a simple stud.

Circular beaded jewellery can be finished with caps for extra decoration before attaching the clasp.

Caps are attached before the clasp and attractively disguise the ends of the threads. They are available in a variety of shapes, sizes and colours and should be matched to the shape, size and colour of the piece of jewellery. Small lightweight caps can be used to finish earrings and also to lengthen and add decoration to a necklace. The caps can also be fitted together against each other and used as extra decoration or to slightly lengthen a piece. A clasp which stands out too much against the beaded work can be blended in by covering it with a filigree cap, or by painting it. The caps are attached to the end of the thread or to the eyepin or headpin. After the cap is attached the threads are finished with a crimp or calotte before the clasp is fitted.

A headpin has a flat top and an eyepin has a small ring or eye at the top. They are available in several sizes in silver or gold from bead shops. Headpins and eyepins link arrangements together with loops— the beads are threaded onto the pins and loops are formed at the end of the pins which are then attached to the piece of jewellery. Beading wire approximately 0.50 mm in silver or gold can be used instead of headpins and eyepins. The pins or a length of beading wire can be bent into shape and attached to the beaded piece with round or flat-nosed pliers and the end cut to size.

Jewellery can also be finished with a calotte or crimp. The calotte is threaded onto the end of the thread with the eye or loop to the side where the clasp is to be attached and closed evenly around the thread with a pair of flat-nosed pliers. The thread is taken back through the hole in the calotte and finished off inside the bead work. For extra security a small amount of glue or clear nail varnish can be applied to the thread.

Calottes and crimps are available from bead shops in silver and gold. Calottes can have open or closed loops. An open loop is attached directly to the clasp, while a closed loop needs a ring before being attached to the clasp. Be sure to close the rings or eyes very carefully to prevent the loss of the jewellery.

As an extra decoration a decorative bead, often a metal or strass bead, can be attached to the finished article before adding the clasp.

5 Flat beading

Beading is the art of using beads threaded onto a piece of cotton or wire to create all sorts of decorative jewellery. Beads can be threaded in any direction or shape and back stitching, done by taking the needle and thread through a previously threaded bead, is frequently employed. Flat beading is done in rows worked forward and backward alternately (similar to knitting). The work is reversed after each row to keep the beads moving continually in the same direction. The beads are attached to the thread one by one. After the required number of beads for the first row have been strung, the beads for the next row are then fastened one by one through a previously attached bead. This creates a strip of connecting beads in a close-fitting pattern. Through the adding on of beads this row will be slightly wider than the first row, which should have been threaded quite loosely. See illustration 3.

This method of beading is very suitable for making wrist bands, watch bands and necklaces. You can use a strong sewing cotton in a colour matching the beads, or a

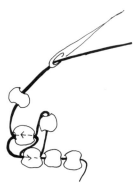

3 *Dividing the work and continuing to bead on the one bead*

thin synthetic natural coloured or black thread. The sewing cotton is thin and supple and forms a practically invisible base for flat beading. Use a double thread, but don't make it too long. A suitable needle can be made from a piece of fine wire (0.15-0.20 mm) approximately 12 cm (5") long, doubled over and twisted around, if you can't buy an appropriate needle.

To commence, thread the first bead to the cotton and fasten with a double knot around the bead (illustration 2). Take the needle through the centre of the bead again to continue the rest of the work from the centre of the bead.

Continue threading the first row. Do make sure before beginning each new row that the thread is going to be long enough to finish that row. All thread ends are knotted at the end of a row to prevent uneven work distorting the pattern of the beads.

The cotton is knotted together with a flat or a double knot, as close as possible against the work. The knots should be invisible and the threads passed back through the beads.

The last thread or end thread is stitched around two or three times and passed back through the beads.

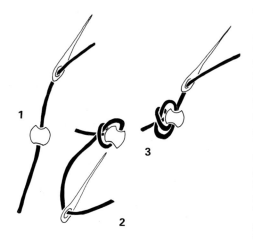

2 *Starting the beadwork with a double knot*

4 *Flat beaded necklace and bracelet (right)*

The beads chosen for this type of flat beading must be uniform in size and shape, as all the beads in the pattern must fit closely together. Round evenly shaped beads or small tube shaped beads are suitable. Very small beads are only suitable if the opening is wide enough to allow the thread to be passed through twice to connect with the previous row. For the most satisfactory effect the beads must be strung together in very neat and regular rows. Occasionally the beading will pull to one side, or the edges will become uneven. This can be remedied by pinning the finished piece to a small piece of chipboard, damping it down slightly and pulling it into shape. Leave to dry.

Flat beading can be worked in any colour combination you choose. Small cross stitch designs provide a ready source of patterns, as each square or cross on the pattern can represent a bead.

The beaded strips can be finished with a small flat clasp or a flat buckle which is fastened to the work with small invisible stitches. You can also use a press stud with a pretty button sewn on top as extra decoration.

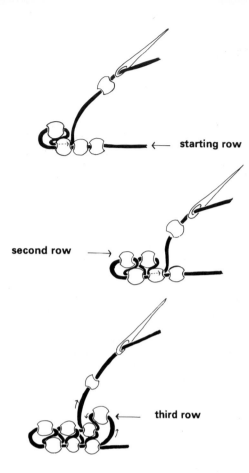

starting row ←

second row →

third row ←

5 *Forward and backward beading*

Necklace
(illustration 4)
You will need
approx. 15 grams small beads (2-3 mm) in
gold (or any colour of your choice)
approx. 150 small beads in a contrasting
colour, e.g. black
a flat clasp

Attach the first gold bead with a double
knot and take the thread back through the
centre of the bead again. Thread two more
beads for the first row. Continue working
backward and forward with the gold beads
until the work measures approximately 15
cm (6"). To make the loops, divide the work
into three strands. Continue working only
with the first bead, adding approximately
20 rows, which measure approximately 4
cm (1 1/2"). Leave the thread long to be
used later.

Attach a new thread to the work and
continue to work with the second bead
(the middle bead) of the necklace. Add
about 25 rows, which measure approximately 5 cm (2") working backward and
forward. Bead back lengthwise with the
black beads, fastening a black bead to the
edge of every third row of the middle
string of beads (see illustration 4). To do
this you thread one black bead and back
stitch through the first two gold beads, add
another black bead to the third gold bead
and bring the needle through. Continue
working this way until the end of the row.
Now continue working on the third bead of
the necklace. Thread about 30 rows,
approximately 6 cm (2 1/4"), working
backward and forward, and thread back
lengthwise with the black beads, attaching
them to the work at every third bead as
before. Thread two black beads and stitch
through the first black bead and through
the lower beads of the work down to the
third lowest bead, adding two black beads
and bringing the needle through. Repeat
to the end of the row and finish the thread
by working it back through the beads.
Continue working with the gold beads and
the thread left over from the first row. Join
the three strings into three loops and join
together. To do this stitch through one
bead of the middle string and one bead of
the third string. Working on these three
beads continue threading backward and
forward for approximately 2 cm (3/4").
Split the string of beads again and work
two more sets of loops with black beads
added as before, plus a middle piece.
Complete the necklace by adding another
15 cm (6") as at the beginning, and finish
off.

6 Simple circular beading

In circular beading the beads are threaded one by one to the cotton. When the first row is completed, each new bead is threaded and then attached to a bead from the previous row. This makes a hollow beaded cord which is very strong because all the beads are connected to each other. A beaded cord is worked in a spiral with each bead threaded singly in the same direction.

Flat beading and simple circular beading are worked quite similarly so that many of the instructions in the previous chapter are also relevant here.

To start, the thread is attached to the first bead with a double knot. The thread is then passed back through the centre of the bead so that the work can be continued from the centre. Thread another 10 beads (a total of 11) and form a circle for the casting on or beginning row, taking the needle through the first joined bead (illustration 6).

To make the next row, the beads are threaded one by one and stitched through. Thread one bead at a time and stitch through the 3rd, 5th, 7th, 9th and 11th beads of the first row.

The third row is begun by stitching into the 1st and 2nd beads of the starting row. Attach the beads one by one to the top beads of the previous row. Continue working all rows this way.

To get an even finish on a circular beaded cord it is advisable to hold the work between thumb and forefinger. At the beginning it is rather difficult to visualise the end result, but after the third or fourth row the beaded cord will start to take shape .

It is easier to use two different colours and an even number of beads. This will create a spiral motif, with the beads being strung in order of colour and back stitched. For example, the starting row could be: 2 white beads, 2 blue beads, 2 white beads, 2 blue beads, 2 white beads, 2 blue beads. Close the circle by stitching through the first white bead. * Thread one blue bead and back stitch through the first following blue bead of the previous row. Thread one white bead and stitch through the first following white bead of the previous row. Repeat from * until the second row is made. Continue to thread bead to bead and colour to colour, stitching through the top beads of the previous row, that is, continue threading one blue bead and stitching through the blue bead of the previous row, then one white bead and stitching through the white bead of the previous row. Continue working in this way until the beaded cord has reached the desired length.

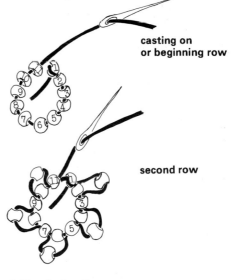

casting on
or beginning row

second row

6 *Circular beading*

There is another way of making a circular beaded cord. Thread and knot the first bead to the cotton and thread on another 5 beads (total of 6 beads). Form a circle for this starting row by passing the needle through the first bead.

From the next row all the beads are threaded and stitched through one by one. Thread one bead at a time and stitch through the 2nd, 3rd, 4th, 5th and 6th beads of the first row. To make the third row stitch through the first bead of the first row and then thread bead by bead in the uppermost beads of the previous row. Continue to make all the following rows in this manner.

An attractive necklace can be made from a circular beaded cord approximately 48 cm (19") long. Make a knot in the middle of the cord and fasten it with a few small invisible stitches to prevent the necklace stretching. Another possibility is to make a single-colour beaded cord (small bugle beads could be used) approximately 50 cm (20") long and a very short but wider piece of beaded cord of approximately 2.5 cm (1") long. Pull the longer beaded cord through the smaller thicker cord and finish the necklace (see illustration 7 opposite).

Beaded cord necklace
(illustration 7)
You will need:
sewing cotton
approx. 30 grams small round regular shaped beads (about 2 mm)
approx. 20 grams medium round regular shaped beads (about 3 mm)
approx. 10 grams large round regular shaped beads (about 4 mm)
approx 10 grams very large round regular shaped beads (about 5 mm)
one clasp

Starting row: 1 small bead, 1 medium bead, 1 small bead, 1 medium bead, 1 small bead, 1 medium bead; close circle by stitching through the first bead.
*Thread one medium bead and stitch

through the medium bead of the starting row. Thread one small bead and stitch through the small bead of the previous row. Repeat from * to complete second row. Then thread bead after bead and stitch through the uppermost bead of the previous row. Continue beading with small and medium beads until work measures approximately 16 cm (6 1/4") For the next 5 cm (2") or so alternate the small beads with the large beads instead of the medium beads.

For the centre piece of the necklace, approximately 3 cm (1 1/4") long, use the extra large beads instead of the large beads. With the small beads then work 5 cm (2") as before using small and large beads.For the last 16 cm (6 1/4") use the small and the medium beads. Finish the necklace.

>7 *Beaded cord necklaces*

Colour photo 1 *Beaded cord necklace and earrings*

7 Beaded loops

The appearance of a circular beaded cord can be transformed with the addition of loops. Following the pattern, extra beads are threaded onto the thread before stitching through a bead from the previous row. To make a beaded cord the beads are threaded one by one and stitched through to the bead from the previous row, but to make a loop several beads at once are threaded and then stitched through a bead from the previous row. This creates a strong beaded cord, alternated with lightweight beaded loops.

A looped cord is worked in a spiral fashion with different sizes and shapes of beads and is always worked in the same direction. The combination of this type of beading and the irregularities of the beads will give the beaded cord a spiral or diabolo effect.

The weight of the beads could cause the nylon thread to stretch or even break. It will depend entirely on the weight of the beaded piece whether to use the thin nylon thread of 0.20 mm or to use the slightly thicker 0.25 mm thread. If necessary a doubled thread could be used, provided the holes in the beads are large enough.

The working thread is usually about 1 metre (40") long. If the thread proves not long enough a new piece may be attached by making two double knots directly against the beads. To attach the new thread take the end of the old thread and the beginning of the new thread between thumb and forefinger. Make a double knot in the two threads, split the two ends, push the knot securely against the beads and make another double knot.

The threads are worked back into the beads. Finishing off joined threads is a fiddly and demanding task, best done immediately rather than leaving it until the work is finished, thus avoiding the risk of distorting the shape of the work. The end of the thread is finished off by sewing it securely two or three times and working it back into the beads.

The beading work needs to be tight and regular. All beads and stitched through beads must fit tightly together, and the thread should not be visible.

If the beading is not tight enough it will tend to look untidy and lose the shape of the spiral and diabolo forms. Don't despair if this happens—a new thread can be strung through the work. Attach the thread and work through the beads one by one and through the centre of the diabolo form, e.g. all the medium sized beads. The beaded cord will become stronger and achieve a better shape, but it may become a little shorter.

This new thread can be used as an extra finishing thread for the calotte or clasp. Longer necklaces need not be finished with a clasp, but you may wish to add some decorative beads at both ends before finishing off. Bracelets use smaller caps and clasps than necklaces. Caps and/ or decorative beads can be attached to the beaded work at the beginning and end of the thread, or attached to an eyepin or headpin. These need to be fastened in the centre of both ends.

Beaded cords can also be finished by attaching a calotte and a crimp at both ends. The clasp is attached to the eye of the calotte.

Beaded cords can occasionally irritate the neck of the wearer, most often because of sharp or rough edges on the beads or because of the weight of the cord. The solution could be to make a shorter beaded cord as a centrepiece and lengthen the necklace with a silk or rayon cord or a metal chain (see colour plate 2 and illustration 16). The accent should still be on the beaded cord, however. The

beaded cord can be finished with a cap at both ends, plus calottes and crimps, and fastened to the silk cord or metal chain. A silk or rayon cord will need to be fastened with tape and a cap. Metal chain can be fastened to the eye of the calotte.
Make sure the fastening is secure and attractive. The amount of beaded work should be balanced against the size of the cord or chain.
A simple rounded or crocheted cord can look very attractive in combination with the larger beaded work. If the beaded work is large enough in diameter a simple cord or crocheted cord could be threaded through it for extra strength. Check the exact length of the necklace before you start to ensure it will fit comfortably and decoratively around the wearer's neck.

The combination of the different beads is very important and very personal and will determine the attractiveness of the end result. Try out the chosen beads first to see if they really go together, perhaps by stringing 20 or 30 on a single thread.
It saves time to collect all the beads and materials together before starting a project. Keep them all together on a serving tray or a large flat lid. The work can then be put away quickly and still remain visibly together.
All the designs described in this book can be made with contrasting colours or with different shades of one colour.
When the instructions stipulate that a different colour, shape or size should be used in a particular pattern, it will be indicated as bead (a) or (b) et cetera. Choice of colours is in most cases left to the reader.

Each beaded piece is started with a bead threaded and knotted with a double knot. Take the thread back through the centre of the bead to enable the work to be continued from the centre of this starting bead. Leave a piece of thread about 15 cm (6") long hanging from the starting bead. Use this later to attach a calotte or clasp.

The beading is done in a spiral, which means row after row is worked in the same direction. A beaded cord can be varied in thickness by varying the number of beads used. Each necklace pattern can also be used to make a bracelet.
The size ratio between large and medium sized beads should be approximately 2:1; this means that the large beads are much larger than the medium beads.

Simple twist necklace
(illustration 8, colour plate 1)
You will need
nylon thread, 0.20 mm
50 grams small beads for the beaded loops (2-3 mm)
600 large beads (4-5 mm)
2 calottes and 2 crimps
2 caps
one clasp

Small round even sized beads are best for this necklace because they are easier to shape. Use a large bead as the starting bead. For the first row thread 1 small, 1 large, 1 small, 1 large and 1 small bead. Close the circle by passing the needle through the large starting bead.
For the second row thread 2 small beads and 1 large bead and stitch through the second large bead of the first row. Continue with 2 small beads and 1 large bead and stitch through the third large bead of the first row. Thread 2 small beads and 1 large bead and stitch through the large starting bead of the first row.
For the third row thread 3 small beads and 1 large bead and stitch through the first large bead of the previous row. Thread 3 small beads and 1 large bead and stitch through the next large bead of the previous row. To finish this row thread 3 small beads and 1 large bead and stitch through the next large bead of the previous row. Repeat this last row until the necklace has

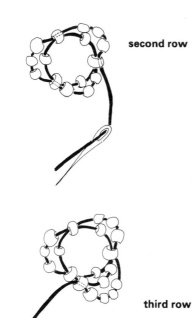

first row

===== stitch through

second row

third row

reached the required length. Decrease the number of beads in the last two rows so this end matches the beginning. For the second last row thread 2 small beads and 1 large bead and stitch through the next large bead of the previous row. For the last row thread 1 small bead and 1 large bead and stitch through the next large bead of the previous row.
Finish the necklace as desired.

Variation of simple twist necklace
Make several twisted cords about 8 cm (3") long, following the above pattern. Join the short cords together to make a necklace.

8 *Simple twist*

^ **Colour photo 2** *Diabolo necklace*
22

> **Colour photo 3** *Necklaces with diabolo design*

Diabolo necklace

(illustration 9 and colour plates 2 and 3)
You will need
nylon thread, 0.20 mm
approx. 30 grams small beads for the
loops (2-3 mm)
approx. 15 grams small bugle beads (2-3
mm)
approx. 200 medium beads
approx. 200 large beads
2 calottes and 2 crimps
2 caps
one clasp

Thread one large bead as the starting
bead.
First row: 1 small bead, 1 bugle bead, 1
medium bead, 1 bugle bead and 1 small
bead. Close the ring by taking the needle
through the large starting bead.
Second row: 2 small beads, 1 bugle bead
and 1 medium bead; stitch through the
medium bead of the previous row.
Continue with 1 bugle bead, 2 small
beads, 1 large bead and stitch through the
large bead of the previous row.
Third row: 3 small beads, 1 bugle bead, 1
medium bead; stitch through the medium
bead of the previous row, thread 1 bugle
bead, 3 small beads, 1 large bead and
stitch through the large bead of the
previous row.
Fourth row: 4 small beads, 1 bugle bead, 1
medium bead; stitch through the medium
bead of the previous row; thread 1 bugle
bead, 4 small beads, 1 large bead and
stitch through the large bead of the
previous row.
Fifth row: 5 small beads, 1 bugle bead, 1
medium bead; stitch through the medium
bead of the previous row; thread 1 bugle
bead, 5 small beads, 1 large bead and
stitch through the large bead of the
previous row.
Sixth row: 6 small beads, 1 bugle bead, 1
medium bead; stitch through the medium
bead of the previous row; thread 1 bugle
bead, 6 small beads, 1 large bead and
stitch through the large bead of the

previous row.
Seventh row: 7 small beads, 1 bugle bead,
1 medium bead; stitch through the
medium bead of the previous row; thread
1 bugle bead, 7 small beads, 1 large bead;
stitch through the large bead of the
previous row.
Repeat this last row until the necklace has
reached the desired length. Then decrease
continually, row by row, with the small
beads (beaded loops), in reverse order to
the earlier described pattern.
Finish the necklace.

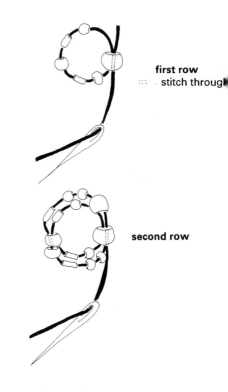

first row
::: stitch throug|

second row

9

24

(Colour plate 4)
You will need
nylon thread, 0.20 mm
1 box small beads (2-3 mm) (a)
1 box small beads (2-3 mm) (b)
1 box small bugle beads
approx. 30 medium beads
approx. 30 large beads
one perforated disc brooch

This is a variation of the diabolo pattern
using two different colours of small beads.
Threading a large bead as a starting bead,
continue beading 1 small bead (a), 1 bugle
bead, 1 medium bead, 1 bugle bead, 1
small bead (b) and close the circle.
Increase each row with the small beads,
and continue until the work fits the
perforated disc of the brooch. The perforated disc can be covered first with a small
piece of fabric in a matching colour.
Sew the beading onto the brooch and
push the beads close together into shape.
Finish the brooch.

Spiral necklace
(illustrations 10 and 11)
You will need
nylon thread, 0.20 mm
approx. 30 grams small beads (2-3 mm) for
the loops
approx. 15 grams small bugle beads (a)
approx. 15 grams small bugle beads (b)
approx. 200 large beads
2 calottes and 2 crimps
2 caps
one clasp

Thread a large bead as starting bead and
continue with 1 bugle (a), 1 bugle (b),1
small bead; close the circle by stitching
through the large starting bead.
Second row: 1 bugle (a) and stitch through
bugle (a) of the previous row, 1 bugle (b)
and stitch through bugle (b) of the previous row; 2 small beads, 1 large bead and
stitch through the large bead of the
previous row.

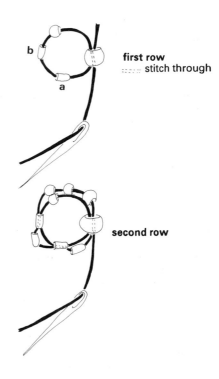

first row
⁚⁚⁚⁚ stitch through

second row

10

Third row: 1 bugle (a) and stitch through
bugle (a) of the previous row, 1 bugle (b)
and stitch through bugle (b) of the previous row; 3 small beads, 1 large bead and
stitch through the large bead of the
previous row.
Continue working in this manner, increasing one small bead in each row, until there
are seven beads in the beaded loops.
Repeat this last row until the desired
length has been reached. Then decrease
row after row with the small beads in the
beaded loops.
Finish the necklace.

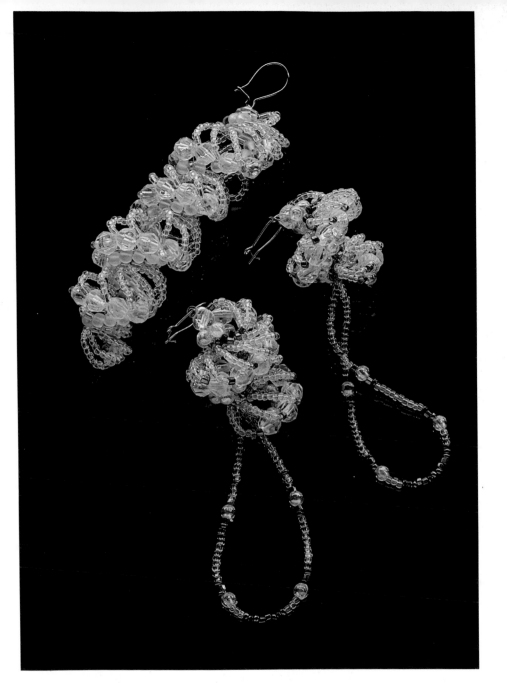

<Colour plate 4 *Necklace, earrings and brooch in spiral beading*

^Colour plate 5 *Earrings in variation of spiral beading*

Earrings, variation of spiral
(illustration 12, colour plate 5)
You will need
nylon thread, 0.20 mm
1 box small beads for beaded loops (2-3 mm)
1 box small bugle beads (a)
1 box small bugle beads (b)
52 medium beads
50 large beads
2 calottes and 2 crimps
2 earring fittings

Thread one large bead as the starting bead, then 1 medium bead, 1 bugle bead (a), 1 bugle bead (b), 10 small beads, 1 bugle bead (a) and close the circle by stitching through the large starting bead.
Second row: 1 medium bead, stitch through medium bead from previous row; 1 bugle bead (a), stitch through bugle bead (a) from previous row; 1 bugle bead (b), stitch through bugle bead (b) from previous row; 10 small beads, 1 bugle bead (a), 1 large bead, stitch through large bead from the previous row.
Repeat this row 23 times and finish with 5 small beads (beaded loop). Finish the earrings.

Necklace, variation of spiral
(colour plate 6)
You will need
nylon thread, 0.20 mm
approx. 20 grams small beads for the beaded loops (2-3 mm)
approx. 15 grams small bugle beads (a)
approx. 10 grams small bugle beads (b)
150 medium beads
150 large beads
50 cm thin cord
2 headpins and 2 caps
one clasp

Thread a large bead as starting bead; 1 medium bead, 1 bugle bead (a), 1 bugle bead (b), 5 small beads, 1 bugle bead (a)

and close the circle by stitching through the starting bead.
Next row: 1 medium bead stitched through the medium bead from the previous row; 1 bugle bead (a) stitched through bugle bead (a) from the previous row; 1 bugle bead (b) stitched through bugle bead (b) from previous row; 10 small beads, 1 bugle bead (a), 1 large bead, stitch through large bead from previous row.
Repeat this row until all the large and medium beads have been used and finish with 5 small beads (beaded loop).
Finish the beaded work and thread the thin cord very carefully through it. Finish the cord and the necklace.

first row
:::::stitch through

second row

12

<11 *Spiral necklaces*

Long bugle bead necklace, stepped
(illustrations 13 and 14)
You will need
nylon thread, 0.20 mm
approx. 20 grams medium beads
approx. 15 grams small beads (a)
approx. 15 grams small bugle beads
approx. 30 grams long bugle beads (about 6 mm)
1 box small beads (b) - the same colour as the long bugle beads
2 calottes and 2 crimps
one clasp

Thread a medium bead as the starting bead; 1 bead (b), 1 bead (a), 1 small bugle bead, 1 bead (b), close the circle by stitching through the medium starting bead.
Second row: 2 beads (b), 1 bead (a) and stitch through bead (a) from the previous row; 1 small bugle bead, stitch through bugle bead from previous row; 2 beads (b), 1 medium bead and stitch through medium bead from previous row.

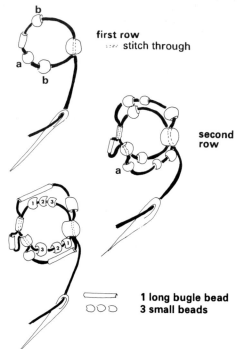

first row
┈┈ stitch through

second row

1 long bugle bead
3 small beads

13

^ **14** *Long bugle bead necklace with central motif, and bracelet in the same style*

>**Colour photo 6** *Variations of the spiral*

Third row: 3 beads (b), 1 bead (a) and stitch through bead (a) from the previous row; 1 small bugle bead and stitch through bugle bead from previous row; 3 beads (b), 1 medium bead and stitch through medium bead from previous row. When the three beads (b) are the same length as the long bugle beads, continue beading with the long bugle beads.

Next row, 1 long bugle bead, 1 bead (a) and stitch through bead (a) from the previous row; 1 small bugle bead and stitch through bugle bead from previous row; 1 long bugle bead, 1 medium bead and stitch through the medium bead from the previous row.

Repeat this row until necklace measures the required length. Finish by working the first 3 rows in reverse order.
Finish the necklace.

Long bugle bead necklace with central motif

Make two pieces approximately 25 cm (10") long and make a brooch in the same colours attached to a perforated disc brooch backing. Very carefully prise off the back of the disc, attach the beaded cords to the sides of the brooch and finish the necklace.

Necklace with pearls

(illustrations 15 and 16)
You will need
nylon thread, 0.20 mm
approx. 30 grams small beads for the beaded loops (2-3 mm)
approx. 10 grams small bugle beads (a)
approx. 10 grams small bugle beads (b)
approx. 400 large pearls (4-5 mm)
2 calottes and 2 crimps
one clasp

Thread one pearl as the starting bead: 1 small bugle bead (a), 1 small bugle bead (b), 3 small beads, 1 small bugle bead (b), 1 small bugle bead (a) and close the circle by stitching through the pearl starting bead.
Second row: 1 small bugle bead (a) and

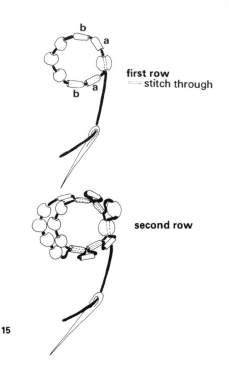

first row
····· stitch through

second row

15

stitch through bugle bead (a) from the previous row; 1 small bugle bead (b) and stitch through bugle bead (b) from the previous row; 4 small beads, 1 small bugle bead (b) and stitch through bugle bead (b) from the previous row; 1 bugle bead (a) and stitch through bugle bead (a) from the previous row; 1 pearl and stitch through pearl from previous row.

Third row: 1 small bugle bead (a) and stitch through bugle bead (a) from the previous row; 1 small bugle bead (b) and stitch through bugle bead (b) from the previous row; 5 small beads, 1 small bugle bead (b) and stitch through bugle bead (b) from the previous row; 1 small bugle bead (a) and stitch through bugle bead (a) from the previous row; 1 pearl and stitch through pearl from the previous row.

Repeat this last row until the necklace reaches the required length. Continue decreasing in each row with the small beads (beaded loops) in reverse order. Finish the necklace.

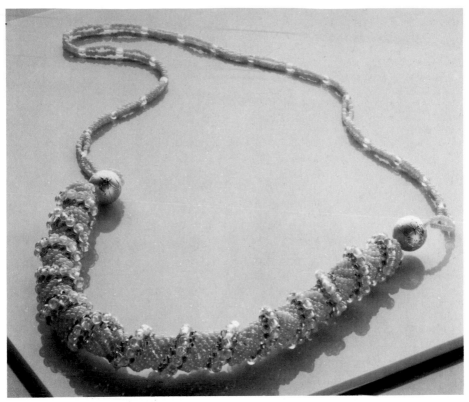

16 *Necklace with pearls*

Necklace with sequins
(illustration 17, colour plate 7)
You will need
nylon thread, 0.20 mm
approx. 50 grams small beads for the
beaded loops
approx. 10 grams small bugle beads (a)
approx. 10 grams small bugle beads (b)
approx. 10 grams small bugle beads (c)
approx. 400 medium beads
2 boxes flat round sequins
2 metal chains approximately 7 cm (2 3/4")
2 calottes and 2 crimps
one clasp

This pattern requires that the thread be
pulled regularly and evenly but not too
tight to prevent the beaded piece from
becoming stiff.

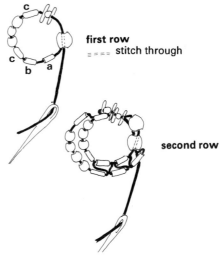

first row
≡ ≡ ≡ ≡ stitch through

second row

17

The abbreviated word combi describes 1 sequin, 1 bugle bead and 1 sequin.

Thread a medium bead as starting bead, 1 bugle bead (a), 1 bugle bead (b), 1 bugle bead (c), 3 small beads, 1 bugle bead (c), 1 combi. Close the circle by stitching through the medium bead (starting bead). Second row: 1 bugle bead (a) and stitch through bugle bead (a) from the previous row; 1 bugle bead (b) and stitch through bugle bead (b) from the previous row; 1 bugle bead (c), 4 small beads, 1 bugle bead (c) and stitch through second bugle bead (c) from the previous row; 1 combi and stitch through combi from previous row, 1 medium bead and stitch through medium bead of previous row.
Third row: 1 bugle bead (a) stitch through bugle bead (a) from previous row; 1 bugle bead (b) stitch through bugle bead (b) from previous row; 1 bugle bead (c) stitch through bugle bead (c) of the previous row (after the 4 small beads); 1 combi stitch through combi from previous row; 1 medium bead stitch through medium bead from previous row.
Repeat this last row until the necklace reaches the required length. Continue decreasing each row with the small beads (beaded loops) reversing the earlier directions for each row.
Finish the necklace and attach the clasp to the ends.

Brooch, large twist
(colour plate 8)
You will need
nylon thread, 0.20 mm
27 large faceted beads (6 mm)
27 large faceted beads (5 mm)
27 medium faceted beads (3 mm)
27 round beads (3 mm)
27 small bugle beads (a)
27 small bugle beads (b)
1 box small beads for the beaded loops (2 mm)
one brooch pin

Thread a large (6 mm) bead as the starting

bead: 1 large bead (5 mm), 1 medium bead, 1 round bead, 1 bugle bead (a), 1 bugle bead (b), 3 small beads and close the circle by stitching through the large 6 mm starting bead.
Second row: 1 large bead (5 mm) stitch through large bead (5 mm) from previous row; 1 medium bead, stitch through medium bead from previous row; 1 round bead, stitch through round bead from previous row; 1 bugle bead (a), stitch through bugle bead (a) from previous row; 1 bugle bead (b), stitch through bugle bead (b) from previous row; 4 small beads, 1 large bead (6 mm), stitch through large bead (6 mm) from previous row.
Repeat this row, increasing one small bead (in the beaded loops) each row, until there are 15 small beads in the beaded loops. Work two more rows with 15 beads in the beaded loops, then decrease one bead in the beaded loops in each row, until there are only 3 small beads left in the beaded loops.
Finish the brooch, sewing the beaded piece to the brooch with invisible stitches.

Lapel or hat pin, large twist
(colour plate 9)
You will need
nylon thread, 0.20 mm
51 faceted beads (6 mm)
51 faceted beads (5 mm)
51 round beads (4 mm)
51 faceted beads (3 mm)
51 round beads (3 mm)
102 small bugle beads (a)
51 small bugle beads (b)
10 grams small beads for the beaded loops
crimp
lapel pin or hat pin

Thread large bead (6 mm) as the starting bead, 1 bead (5 mm), 1 round bead (4 mm), 1 bead (3 mm), 1 round bead (3 mm), 2 bugle beads (a), 1 bugle bead (b), 1 small bead, and close the circle by stitching through the large bead (6 mm).

18 *Necklace with large twist*

^ **Colour plate 8** *Brooches with large twist*
< **Colour plate 7** *Necklaces with sequins*

Second row: 1 bead (5 mm), stitch through bead (5 mm) from previous row; 1 round bead (4 mm), stitch through round bead (4 mm) from previous row; 1 bead (3 mm), stitch through bead (3 mm) from previous row; 1 round bead (3 mm), stitch through round bead (3 mm) from previous row; 1 bugle (a), stitch through first bugle (a) from previous row; 1 bugle (a), stitch through second bugle (a) from previous row; 1 bugle (b), stitch through bugle (b) from previous row; 1 small bead, 1 large bead (6 mm), stitch through large bead (6 mm) from previous row.

Repeat this row three more times, then continue working but increasing 1 small bead in the beaded loops each row until there are 21 beads in each beaded loop. Repeat the last row twice. Then continue working but decreasing one small bead each row until there is only one bead left in the beaded loops. Repeat this last row four times.

Finish the beading.

Attach a decorative bead to the top of the lapel or hat pin. Push the beaded work onto the pin and squeeze a crimp up against the work to prevent it slipping down.

Large twist necklace
(illustration 18)
You will need
nylon thread, 0.20 mm
63 large beads (4 mm) (a)
63 large beads (4 mm) (b)
63 faceted beads (4 mm) (c)
126 small bugle beads (d)
63 small bugle beads (e)
63 small bugle beads (f)
126 small bugle beads (g)
approx. 20 grams small beads for the beaded loops
approx. 20 grams small bugle beads (f)
buttonhole silk
one clasp

Thread a large bead (a) as the starting bead, 1 bead (b), 1 bead (c), 2 bugles (d), 1 bugle (e), 1 bugle (f), 2 bugles (g), 3 small beads and close circle by stitching through large bead (a).

Second row: 1 bead (b), stitch through bead (b) from previous row; 1 bead (c), stitch through bead (c) from previous row; 1 bugle (d), stitch through first bugle (d) from previous row; 1 bugle (d), stitch through second bugle (d) from previous row; 1 bugle (e), stitch through bugle (e) from previous row; 1 bugle (f), stitch through bugle (f) from previous row; 1 bugle (g), stitch through first bugle (g) from previous row; 1 bugle (g), stitch through second bugle (g) from previous row; 5 small beads, 1 bead (a), stitch through bead (a) from previous row.

Repeat this row, increasing 2 small beads in the beaded loops in each row until there are 21 small beads in each beaded loop. Repeat this last row 44 times, then decrease 2 small beads in each row until there are 3 small beads left in each beaded loop.

Finish the beading work.

Make a thin beaded cord of small bugle beads (f) about 50 cm (20") long. Very carefully pull this beaded cord through the loosely beaded piece.

Finish the necklace.

8 Other beading

There are many other ways of using beads to create handmade fashion jewellery—earrings, brooches and collars, for example.

Earrings, bead balls
(illustration 19)
You will need
nylon thread, 0.20 mm
2 transparent (faceted) synthetic beads
(approximately 2 cm)
1 box small beads
1 box sequins
112 large beads
2 calottes and 2 crimps
2 earring fittings or clips

Beads used in earrings should be as lightweight as possible.
The synthetic beads which are very light are used as the centre around which the beads and the sequins are beaded. The hole in the centre of the bead is used as the central point of the work and the beading is worked from left to right.
Work with a long thread and adjust the number of small beads according to the size of the synthetic bead.
The word combi is used for a combination of 1 sequin, 1 small bead and 1 sequin.
Series is used for 1 sequin, 1 small bead, 1 sequin, 1 small bead and 1 sequin.

Thread the synthetic bead as the starting bead and work row after row around the bead, moving from top to bottom and from left to right.
Row 1: 1 large bead, 5 small beads, 1 large bead, 1 combi, 1 large bead, 5 small beads, 1 large bead, 1 series, 1 large bead, take needle (from bottom to top) through the centre of the synthetic bead.
Row 2: take needle through first bead from previous row. Thread 5 small beads, 1 large bead, 1 combi, 1 large bead, 5 small

take needle through centre of synthetic bead.
Row 3: 1 large bead, 5 small beads, 1 large bead, 1 combi, 1 large bead, 1 combi, 1 large bead, 5 small beads, take needle through last beaded large bead, series and large bead from the previous row. Take needle through centre of synthetic bead.
Row 4: take needle through the first large bead from previous row, 5 small beads, 1 large bead, 1 combi, 1 large bead, 5 small beads, 1 large bead, 1 series, 1 large bead, take needle through centre of synthetic bead.
Repeat rows 3 and 4 until you have 8 double loops. Finish with row 3 and stitch through the large bead, series and the large bead from the first row. Finish the bead ball.

19

Necklace, variation of bead ball
Bead five bead balls and six pieces of beaded cord following the instructions for the simple twist (see page 21) and attach the bead balls between the beaded cords. Finish necklace.

Colour photo 9 *Lapel pins or hat pins*

>**Colour photo 10** *Beaded loop earrings*

40

Beaded loop earrings

(illustration 20, colour plate 10)
You will need
nylon thread, 0.20 mm
1 box small beads
40 oval beads
20 large bugle beads
80 faceted beads (3 mm)
30 large beads (5 mm)
2 caps, 2 eyepins and 2 crimps
2 earring fittings or hangers

Beading even loops is made much easier when you use a cardboard guide. Make this from a piece of cardboard 6 cm (2 1/2") square with two holes pierced in it (see illustration 20). Thread a doubled piece of nylon thread about 30 cm (12") long through the holes (these are called the helplines); take the thread through the hole on the right and bring it to the front. Knot the threads with a single knot and stick the knot down at the back of the cardboard with a piece of tape.
Combi refers to 1 bead (3 mm),1 large bead and 1 bead (3 mm).

Thread 8 small beads, 1 oval bead, 1 bead (3 mm), 1 oval bead, 5 small beads, 1

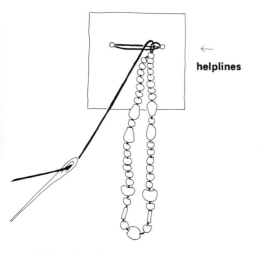

20 *Cardboard guide with helplines*

combi, 1 bugle, 1 combi, 1 bugle, 1 combi, 5 small beads, 1 oval bead, 1 bead (3 mm), 1 oval bead and 7 small beads. To close the loop, stitch through first small bead from bottom to top and under the helpline. Bead 4 more loops, then take the thread back through the right hole. Remove the tape from the back of the cardboard and release the knot. All threads are now double knotted and finished with a crimp. Finish earrings as required.

Earrings

(illustration 21)
You will need
nylon thread, 0.20 mm
1 box small beads
12 faceted beads (3 mm)
4 faceted beads (4 mm)
2 faceted beads (5 mm)
2 faceted beads (6 mm)
4 small round strass beads
2 calottes and 6 crimps
2 earring fittings or hangers

This pattern is worked using one thread approximately 60 cm (24") long, but both ends are used.
Thread a calotte and a crimp into the centre of the thread, bringing the thread back through the crimp. Squeeze the crimp flat and the calotte closed with a pair of flat-nosed pliers.
The calotte could be attached to a piece of chipboard with a pin, which will make it easier to bead evenly. There are now two working threads, a left thread and a right thread. When a bead is threaded on the left thread the right thread is used to stitch through that bead from bottom to top, which causes the threads to cross auto-matically, the left thread becoming the right thread and vice versa.You will need two needles.
With both threads together thread 1 large bead (3 mm), 1 strass bead and 1 large bead (3 mm). Separate the threads. On the left thread 3 small beads, 1 large bead (3 mm); on the right thread 3 small beads, and take the needle from bottom to

top through the large bead (3 mm) of the left thread.

Pull on the threads lightly to even the work.

On the left thread 5 small beads, 1 large bead (3 mm); on the right thread 5 small beads. Take needle from bottom to top through the large bead (3 mm) of the left thread.

On the left thread 5 small beads, 1 large bead (4 mm); on the right thread 5 small beads. Take needle from bottom to top through the large bead (4 mm) of the left thread.

On the left thread 5 small beads, 1 large bead (4 mm); on the right 5 small beads. Take the needle from bottom to top through the large bead (4 mm) of the left thread.

On the left thread 5 small beads, 1 large bead (5 mm); on the right thread 5 small beads. Take needle from bottom to top through the large bead (5 mm) of the left thread.

On the left thread 7 small beads, 1 large bead (6 mm); on the right thread 7 small beads. Knot the two threads carefully together and work the ends into the beads. Attach a crimp to the bottom of the earring and close it. Thread onto the hanger the beaded earring, 1 large bead (3 mm), 1 strass bead, 1 large bead (3 mm) and 1 crimp and close it. The earring and beaded decoration will be securely attached.

1

2

Colour photo 11 *Bracelet, necklace and earrings*

>**Colour photo 12** *Pierrot neckpiece*

44

Bracelet

(illustration 22, colour plate 11)

You will need

nylon thread, 0.20 mm
57 faceted beads (4 mm)
2 long decorative beads or strass beads
1 box small beads
2 calottes and 2 crimps
one clasp

This pattern uses two threads, each approximately 1 m (1 yard) long, and all four ends are used for beading.

With the two threads together thread a calotte and a crimp into the middle. Pull the threads back through the calotte (illustration 22-1), pinch the crimp and close the calotte. Attach the calotte with a pin to a piece of chipboard, which will make it easier to bead evenly.

There are four working threads. Thread one of the large decorative beads through all four threads. From this point use only two threads for beading, a left thread and a right thread. The other two threads will

be used later for threading with the small beads. You will need two needles.

On the left thread string 2 beads (4 mm); on the right thread 1 bead (4 mm), as in (illustration 22-2). Take needle from bottom to top through the second bead of the left thread (illustration 22-3). Gently pull the threads to even the work. The threads cross over automatically, the left thread becoming the right thread and vice versa. Repeat this row until all the beads have been used, leaving 1 bead on the left thread and 1 bead on the right thread.

With both threads together thread one large decorative bead, a calotte and a crimp. Take the threads back through the calotte but don't close the calotte or the crimp yet as you will continue working with the two leftover threads and the small beads, which are evenly beaded over the large beads.

With both threads together thread 2 small beads, then separate the threads. Thread 2 beads onto the left thread and take

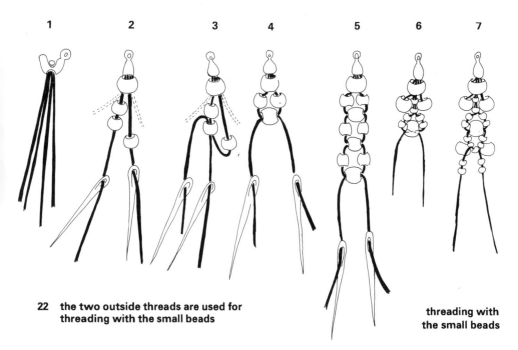

1   **2**   **3**   **4**   **5**   **6**   **7**

22 the two outside threads are used for
threading with the small beads

threading with
the small beads

46

the needle from left to right through the first large bead; thread 2 small beads to the right thread and take the needle from right to left through the same large bead. The threads will automatically cross over, after they have been gently pulled tight. Thread 3 small beads on to the left thread and 2 small beads on to the right thread, take needle from bottom to top through the fourth (second last) small bead of the left thread.

Continue working these last two rows alternately, finishing with 2 small beads on the left thread and 2 small beads on the right thread. Hold the threads together and thread 2 small beads.

Thread both threads together through the large decorative bead, the calotte and the crimp, then back through the calotte again. Pinch the crimp and close the calotte. Finish the bracelet.

Lizard brooch

(illustrations 23 and 24, colour plate 13)
You will need
nylon thread, 0.25 mm

1 box medium beads (3-4 mm) (a)
27 medium beads (b)
2 medium beads (c)
one brooch back with pin

This pattern is worked with a long thread of about 1 m (1 yard), with both ends being used for threading. The pattern will be beaded twice, once for the front and once for the back. The pattern is worked row after row from top to bottom.

Thread 1 bead (a) in the middle of the thread. This will give you two working threads, a left and a right, making it necessary to use two needles. After each beaded and stitched row the work is reversed and continued in the same manner as before. All rows from the 2nd row to the 23rd row are repeated. Thread 2 beads (a) on to the left thread and take the other thread through these 2 beads from left to right. Thread 3 beads (a) and take the needle with the right thread from left to right

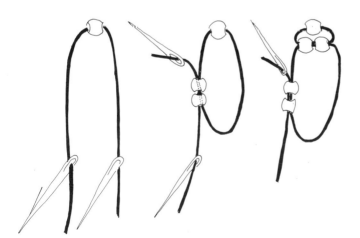

23

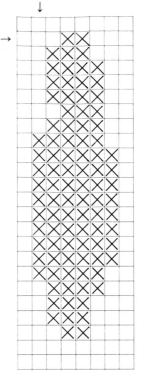

back

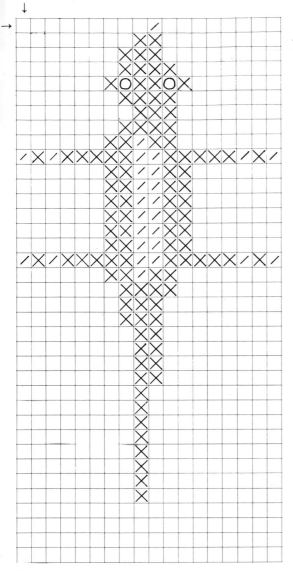

front

 = a
／ = b
○ = c

24 *Pattern for lizard*

<**Colour photo 13** *Lizard brooches*

through these 3 beads. Reverse the work
and repeat this row for the back.
Thread 4 beads (a) on to left thread and
take the needle with the right thread from
left to right through these 4 beads. Reverse
the work and repeat this row.
Thread on to left thread 1 bead (a), 1 bead
(c), 2 beads (a), 1 bead (c), 1 bead (a), take
the needle from the right thread from left
to right only through the 4 beads (a). The
beads (c) form the eyes and will be raised
slightly above the other beads. Reverse
the work, thread 4 beads (a) and take the
needle through these beads.
Continue working in this way, following the
pattern till row 10. Thread on to left thread
for the body, 2 beads (a), 2 beads (b), 2
beads (a), for the leg 3 beads (a), 1 bead
(b), 1 bead (a) and 1 bead (b). Take the
needle with the left thread from left to
right through the 3 beads (a) and the
needle with the right thread from left to
right through the 6 beads of the body.
Reverse the work and repeat this row,
using only beads (a) for the back of the
body.
Continue working as the pattern and
thread row 17 in the same manner as row
10. From row 23 only the front is worked.
Finish the lizard and sew the brooch back
to the back with invisible stitches.

Simple collar
(illustrations 25 and 26)
You will need
silk thread the same colour as the beads
approx. 550 medium beads (3-4 mm)
2 decorative beads
1 box small beads
2 calottes and 2 crimps
one clasp

Thread a calotte and crimp to the end of
the thread. Pinch the crimp and the calotte
very carefully closed.
Because in this pattern the thread stays
visible the colour should match the beads
closely.
Attach the calotte with a pin to a piece of
chipboard.

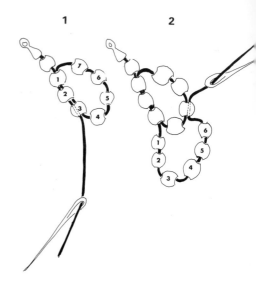

25

The collar is worked from left to right,
keeping the beading regular and even.
Thread a decorative bead then 7 medium
beads, and close the circle by taking the
needle through the 1st, 2nd and 3rd bead
(see illustration 25-1). Thread 6 medium
beads and take the needle from bottom to
top through the 5th bead of the first row
(see illustration 25-2). Thread 4 medium
beads and take the needle from top to
bottom through the 6th bead of the
previous row (see illustration 25-3).
Thread 2 medium beads and 1 small bead.
take the needle from bottom to top
through the 2nd bead (see illustration 25-
4). Thread 3 medium beads and take the
needle from bottom to top through the 3rd
bead of the previous row.
Thread 4 medium beads and take the
needle from top to bottom through the
2nd large bead (which is actually the 4th
bead) of the previous row (see illustration
25-5).

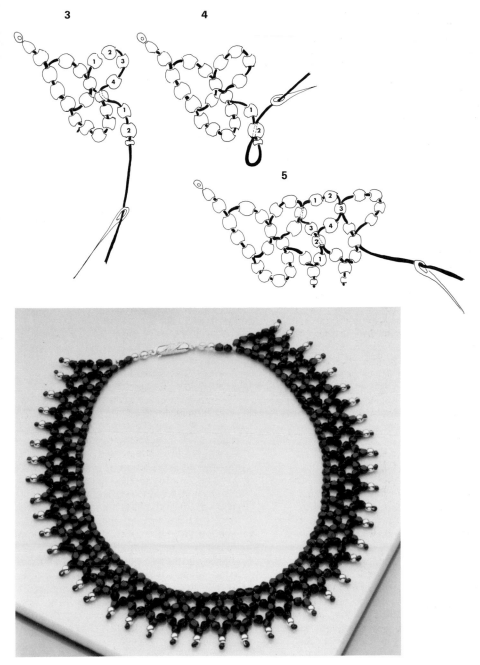

26 *Simple collar*

Continue working these 2 rows alternately until the collar has reached the desired length, finishing with a second row. Thread 6 medium beads and take the needle from bottom to top through the 3rd bead of the previous row.

Continue with 5 medium beads and take the needle from top to bottom through the 5th, 4th, 3rd, 2nd and 1st beads of the previous row.

Take the needle through the other beads until the thread reaches the end of the collar.

Thread a decorative bead, a calotte and a crimp and take the thread back through the calotte. Pinch the crimp and close the calotte very carefully. Finish the collar.

Pierrot neckpiece

(illustration 27, colour plate 12)
You will need
silk thread
50 grams medium beads (3-4 mm)
30 grams small beads (2 mm) (a)
30 grams small beads (2 mm) (b)
30 grams small beads (2 mm) (c)
4 calottes and 4 crimps
one clasp

The first step in making this neckpiece is to make a base to which the loops of beads will be attached. The beadwork in this base should not be tight, but must be very regular and even. When you are selecting the medium beads for the base choose some with a large hole in the centre, because they will be stitched through several times. Also take into consideration that the base may become a little shorter once the loops are beaded onto it.

The beading is done from left to right. Two special terms need explanation. A standing bead is a bead whose hole runs vertically after it has been beaded and stitched through. A laying bead is a bead whose hole runs horizontally after it has been beaded and stitched through.

Thread a calotte and a crimp and take the thread back through the calotte. Attach the calotte with a pin to a piece of chipboard. This will make it easier to bead in an even regular manner.

First row: thread 5 beads and close the circle by taking the needle from right to left through the 2nd and 3rd beads (see illustration 27-1).

Next row: thread 3 beads and take the needle from bottom to top through the 4th bead of the previous row and from right to left through the 1st bead of this new row (see illustration 27-2).

Third row: thread 3 beads and take needle from bottom to top through the 2nd bead of the previous row and from right to left through the 1st bead of this new row (see illustration 27-3).

Repeat this last row until the necklace has reached the desired length of about 47 cm (18 1/2") and finish with 1 bead, 1 calotte and a crimp. Take the thread back through the calotte.

Take a new thread. Thread a calotte and a crimp and take the thread back through the calotte. Attach the calotte to the piece of chipboard directly under the calotte of the 1st row.

Second row: thread 4 beads and take needle from right to left through the first laying bead of the 1st circle of the 1st row. (see illustration 27-4)

Thread 3 beads and take the needle from right to left through the first laying bead, where the thread comes out before the new beads were threaded, and from right to left through the following bead of the previous row (see illustration 27-5)

Thread 2 beads and take the needle from bottom to top through the first standing bead of the previous group and from right to left through the first following laying bead and the following laying bead of the previous row (see illustration 27-6)

Repeat this last row to the end of the work and finish with 3 beads, 1 calotte and 1 crimp. Take the thread back through the calotte.

first row

1

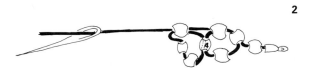

2

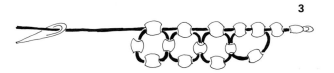

3

second row

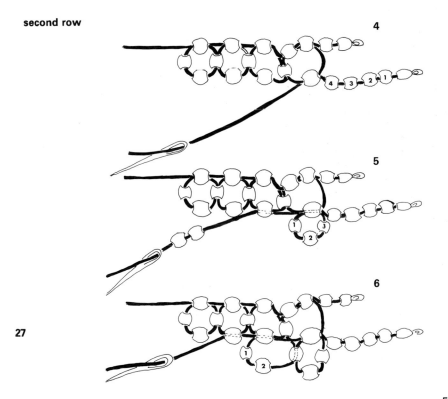

4

5

6

27

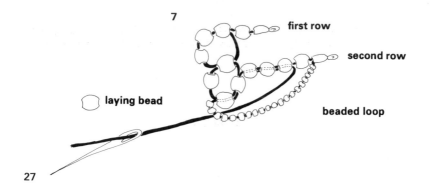

7

first row

second row

laying bead

beaded loop

27

Now the loops with the small beads will be threaded. They will overlay each other and are then stitched to the base.
Attach a new thread through the calotte of the 2nd row. Take needle from left to right through the calotte and the crimp and then back again through the calotte.
Make the first row of beaded loops with small beads (a). Thread 20 small beads and take the needle from left to right back through the first laying bead, and the 4th, 3rd and 2nd bead from the start of the 2nd row (see illustration 27-7).
Thread 20 small beads and take the needle from left to right back through the following and previous laying beads, the previous standing bead and the 4th bead from the beginning of the 2nd row.
Thread 20 small beads and take the needle from left to right back through the following and previous laying beads of the 2nd row.
Continue working in this manner, threading the beaded loops to the end of the 2nd row of the base. Finish in reverse order of the described pattern. Finish the thread in the calotte and crimp.

Make the second row of beaded loops using small beads (b). Attach a new thread to the calotte in the 2nd row of the base. Very carefully close the crimp and the calotte.
Start threading similarly to the first row of beaded loops —thread 20 small beads

and take the needle back from left to right through the 3rd, 2nd and 1st laying beads of the 2nd row.Thread 20 small beads and take the needle back from left to right through the 4th, 3rd and 2nd laying beads of the 2nd row, and so on to the end.
The beaded loops will be slightly longer than the loops of the first row. Thread the beaded loops to the end of the 2nd row of the base. Finish in reverse order the pattern for the 1st row. Finish the thread in the calotte and the crimp, carefully closing both.
Make the 3rd row of beaded loops using small beads (c). Attach a new thread to the calotte of the 1st row of the base. Close the crimp and the calotte very carefully.
Thread 20 beads and take the needle back from left to right through the 2nd and 1st laying beads of the 1st row.
Thread 20 beads and take the needle back from left to right through the 3rd and the 2nd laying beads of the 1st row and so on to the end.
Thread the beaded loops to the end of the 1st row of the base.
Finish the thread in the calotte and the crimp of the 1st row and close the calotte and crimp carefully.
Finish the necklace.

In conclusion , I wish everyone who with the help of this book has made beaded jewellery much pleasure. Let the beads be your inspiration.

LACIS publishes and distributes books specifically related to the textile arts, focusing on the subjects of lace and lace making, costume, embroidery, needlepoint and hand sewing.

Other LACIS books of interest:

BEAD EMBROIDERY, Joan Edwards
EMBROIDERY WITH BEADS, Angela Thompson
BEAD EMBROIDERY, Valerie Campbell-Harding & Pamela Watts
THE BEADING BOOK, Julia Jones
BEAD WORK, ed by Jules & Kaethe Kliot
BEADED ANIMALS IN JEWELRY, Latty Lammens & Els Scholte
HAUTE COUTURE EMBROIDERY, THE ART OF LESAGE, Palmer White
THE ART OF TATTING, Katherine Hoare
TATTING WITH VISUAL PATTERNS, Mary Konior
TATTING; Designs from Victorian Lace, ed by Jules & Kaethe Kliot
THE COMPLETE BOOK OF TATTING, Rebecca Jones
NEW DIMENSIONS IN TATTING, To de Haan-van Beek
THE BARGELLO BOOK, Frances Salter
FLORENTINE EMBROIDERY, Barbara Muller
THE NEEDLE MADE LACE OF RETICELLA, ed by Jules & Kaethe Kliot
THE ART OF SHETLAND LACE, Sarah Don
KNITTED LACE, Marie Niedner & Gussi von Reden
THE MAGIC OF FREE MACHINE EMBROIDERY, Doreen Curran
THE CARE AND PRESERVATION OF TEXTILES, Karen Finch & Greta Putnam
MILLINERY FOR EVERY WOMAN, Georgina Kerr Kaye
"STANDARD" WORK ON CUTTING (MEN'S GARMENTS): 1886
LADIES' TAILOR-MADE GARMENTS 1908, S.S. Gordon
THE ART & CRAFT OF RIBBON WORK, ed by Jules & Kaethe Kliot
BEADS IN TATTING, Judith Connors
TAMBOUR WORK, Yusai Fukuyama
BERLIN WORK, SAMPLERS & EMBROIDERY, Raffaella Serena
CLASSIC BEADED PURSE PATTERNS, Jong-Kramer
HUCK EMBROIDERY, Ondori Staff
THE MARY FRANCES SEWING BOOK, Jane Eayre Fryer

For a complete list of LACIS titles write to:

LACIS
3163 Adeline Street
Berkeley, CA 94703
USA